Mystery Ancestor

Heather Hammonds

★Family Members★

Emma
Benjamin
June
James
Peter
Caroline
Rachel
Stephen

- Mom
- Dad
- Grandma - Mom's mom
- Grandpa - Mom's dad
- Pop - Dad's dad
- Nanna - Dad's mom
- Mom's sister
- Mom's brother
- Mom's nie

Rigby®

Tom and I have found a very old photo of someone.

Is it one of our ancestors?

The members of your family who lived long ago are your **ancestors**.

Sometimes your ancestors look like you or another member of your family. You might have the same color hair or eyes or the same shaped nose.

There are lots of people in our family. Where do we start looking?

This person is studying her family history.

Many people study their family history.
They learn:

- ▶ What their ancestors' names were
- ▷ When their ancestors lived and died
- ▶ What jobs their ancestors did
- ▷ How many children their ancestors had

The study of family history is called **genealogy**. People who study family history are called **genealogists**.

You can learn about your family history. Find out:

▶ The names of your ancestors

▶ When your ancestors lived and died

▶ If your ancestors were married

▶ If your ancestors had children

Look at old family photographs and **diaries**.
Try to find out who the people are in the
photographs. Ask your family to help you.

We were stuck. There were no more clues in the photo album.

Try the genealogical society.

Is our mystery ancestor our great-great-grandmother?

You can find information on the Internet and at some large libraries. You can also find information at a genealogical society.

At a genealogical society, genealogists will help you:

▶ Find information about your family history

▶ Write about your family history

We needed to find out if Constance was our great-great-grandmother.

You can visit a special government office for more information. Ask for a copy of your great-grandmother's death certificate and a copy of your great-great-grandmother's birth certificate.

A birth certificate

Sometimes you can find more information from special government offices. The offices keep **records** of births, deaths, and marriages for people in their area.

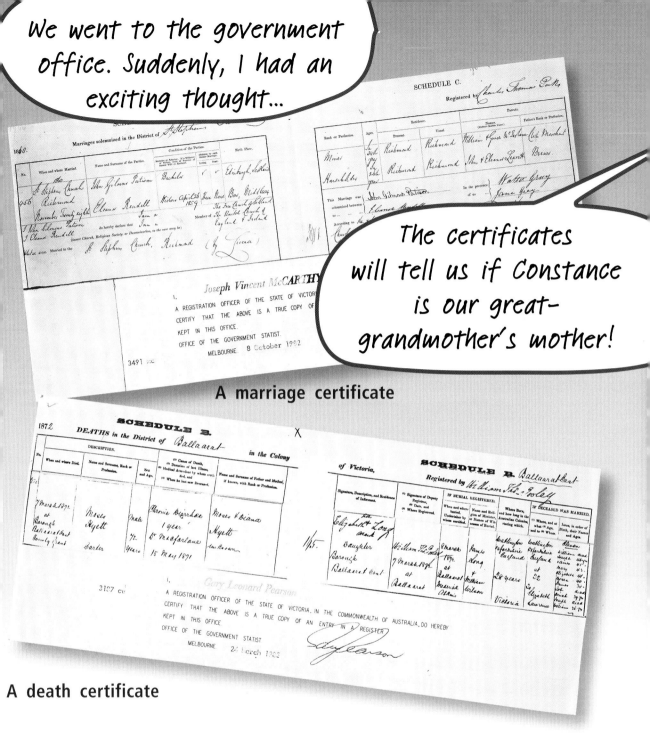

A marriage certificate

A death certificate

You can get **certificates** that show you when your ancestors were born, when they got married, and when they died.

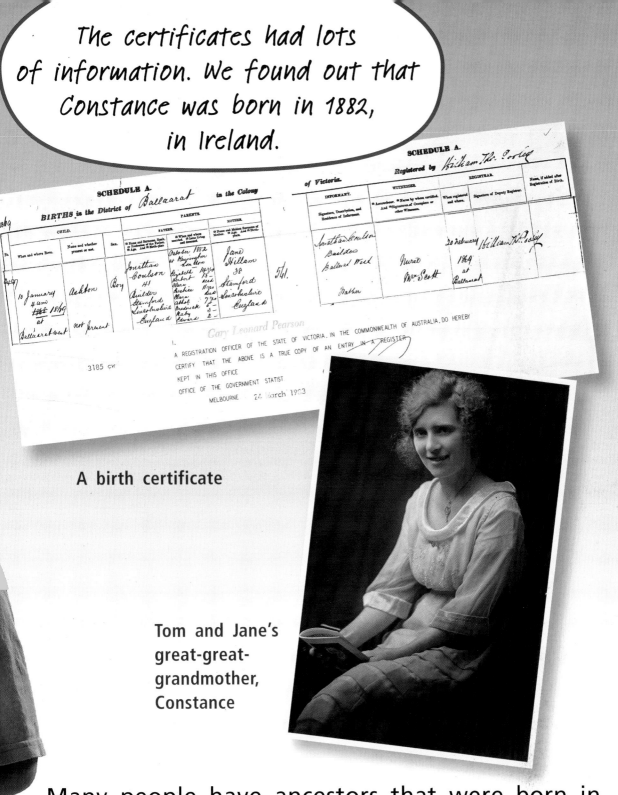

> The certificates had lots of information. We found out that Constance was born in 1882, in Ireland.

A birth certificate

Tom and Jane's great-great-grandmother, Constance

Many people have ancestors that were born in another country. Often, these ancestors moved to the country that you were born in.

Look! Constance married a man named Thomas, who was our great-great-grandfather!

Wow! Maybe I'm named after Thomas. My name is Tom, too! Constance and Thomas had two children.

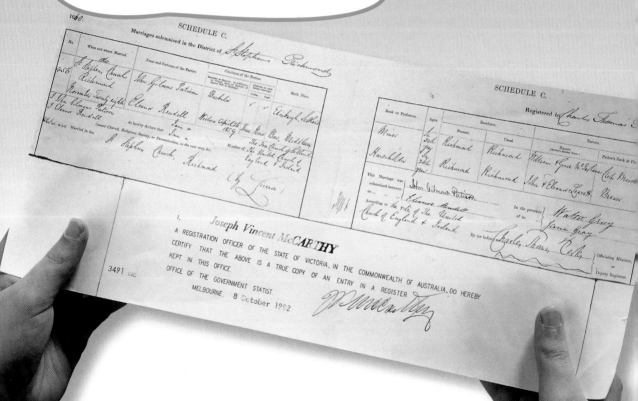

The certificates can also help you find out how many children your ancestors had.

Our family history mystery was solved! We learned lots of other things about Constance and Thomas. Thomas was a sailor. Constance worked at home, looking after the house and the children.

Constance and Thomas had two children.

Tom and Jane's great-great grandfather, Thomas

42 BOURKE S⊥ EAST
MELBOURNE.

You can find out what sort of jobs your ancestors did.

There was more information on the death certificate. Constance died in 1969. Thomas died in 1957. They were buried in Greenwood Cemetery.

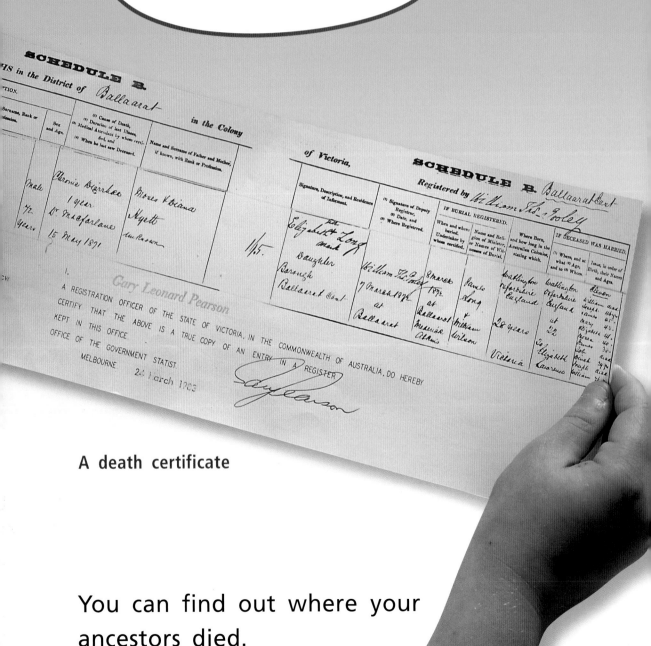

A death certificate

You can find out where your ancestors died.

You can even visit your family's **gravestones** at cemeteries.

Sometimes people make special lists of information about their ancestors. The lists show the births, deaths, and marriages of ancestors. They also show how many children they had and how ancestors are related to each other.

Make a pedigree chart or a family tree chart.

What a great idea!

A **pedigree chart** is a list that looks like this.

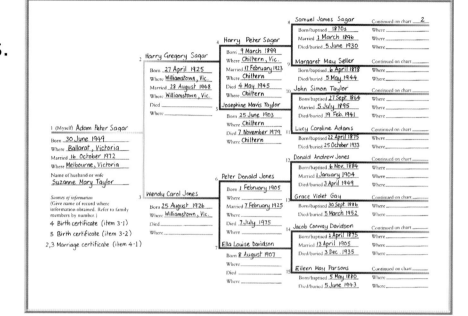

A **family tree chart** is a list that looks like this.

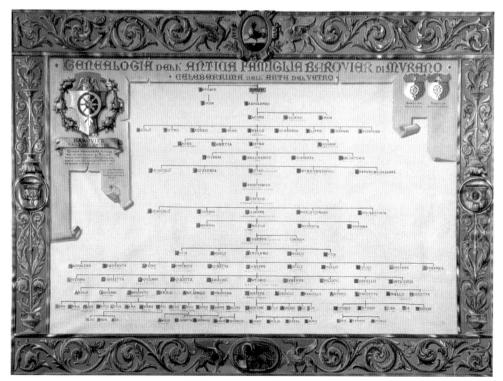

We decided to make a family tree chart to show our family history.

1 Draw a tree on a large sheet of paper.
At the bottom of the tree draw a leaf. Write your name and date of birth in the leaf. If you have any brothers or sisters, do the same for them as well.

2 Above your leaf, draw leaves for each of your parents. Write their names and dates of birth in the leaves.

3 Above your parents' leaves, draw leaves for your grandparents. Write their names and dates of birth in the leaves.

4 Keep drawing leaves for your great-grandparents and great-great-grandparents, if you can!

Patrick Taylor
b. May 9, 1914
d. _____

Sarah Thomas
b. April 8, 1909
d. June 6, 1996

May Simmons
b. January 2, 1911
d. April 22, 1995

Donald Wilson
b. June 5, 1909
d. May 29, 2001

Peter Taylor
b. September 5, 1928
d. _____

Caroline Wilson
b. January 22, 1930
d. _____

Benjamin Taylor
b. August 7, 1964
d. _____

Tom Taylor
b. June 16, 1994
d. _____

Our Family Tree

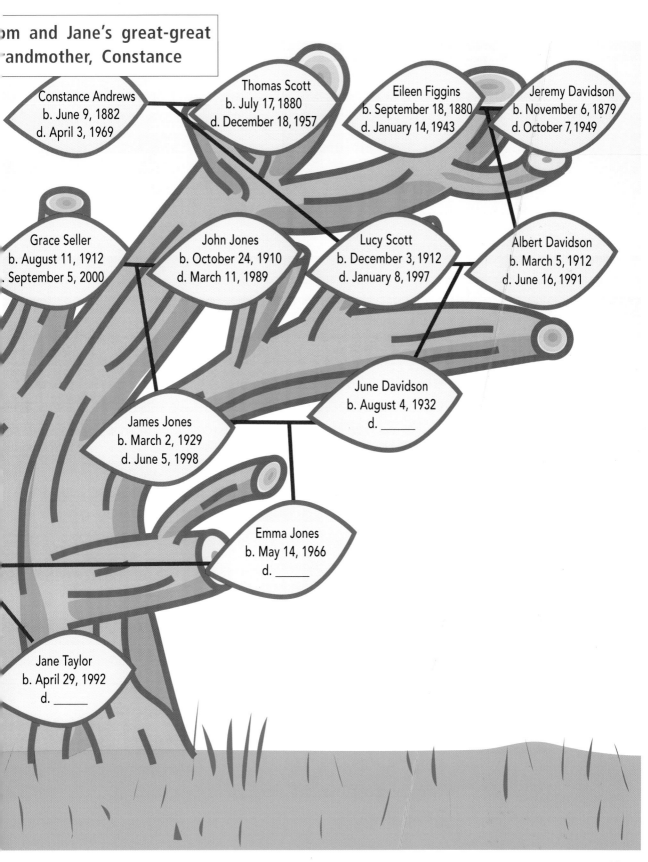

Constance Andrews
b. June 9, 1882
d. April 3, 1969

Thomas Scott
b. July 17, 1880
d. December 18, 1957

Eileen Figgins
b. September 18, 1880
d. January 14, 1943

Jeremy Davidson
b. November 6, 1879
d. October 7, 1949

Grace Seller
b. August 11, 1912
. September 5, 2000

John Jones
b. October 24, 1910
d. March 11, 1989

Lucy Scott
b. December 3, 1912
d. January 8, 1997

Albert Davidson
b. March 5, 1912
d. June 16, 1991

June Davidson
b. August 4, 1932
d. _____

James Jones
b. March 2, 1929
d. June 5, 1998

Emma Jones
b. May 14, 1966
d. _____

Jane Taylor
b. April 29, 1992
d. _____

Glossary

ancestors members of your family who lived long ago

certificate a written document that states something to be a fact. A birth certificate tells you when and where someone was born.

diaries books that contain a record of events that happen in a person's life

family tree chart a special chart, often shaped like a tree, showing many members of a family

genealogy the study of family history

genealogists people who study family history

gravestones stones put on top of the place where a person is buried. Gravestones have the date of birth and the date of death of a perso on them.

pedigree chart a special chart that reads from left to right, showing many members of a family

records written reports that have information on them

Index

24